D0762568

Gallery Books
Editor: Peter Fallon

THE MAGDALENE SERMON

Eiléan Ní Chuilleanáin

THE
MAGDALENE
SERMON

Gallery Books

The Magdalene Sermon
is first published
simultaneously in paperback
and in a clothbound edition
on 10 November 1989.

The Gallery Press
Loughcrew
Oldcastle
County Meath
Ireland

All rights reserved

© Eiléan Ní Chuilleanáin 1989

ISBN 1 85235 050 4 (*paperback*)
1 85235 051 2 (*clothbound*)

Acknowledgements are made to the editors of the following:
*Aquarius, Broadsheet, Concerning Poetry, Cyphers, Gown, An Muinteoir,
Orbis, Poetry Ireland Review, Poets for Africa, Verse* and *Wildish Things*
(Attic Press) in which some of these poems have been published.
   The Gallery Press receives financial assistance from An
Chomhairle Ealaíon / The Arts Council, Ireland.

Contents

in loving memory of
Katherine Kavanagh
1928-1989

Pygmalion's Image

Not only her stone face, laid back staring in the ferns,
But everything the scoop of the valley contains begins to move
(And beyond the horizon the trucks beat the highway.)

A tree inflates gently on the curve of the hill;
An insect crashes on the carved eyelid;
Grass blows westward from the roots,
As the wind knifes under her skin and ruffles it like a book.

The crisp hair is real, wriggling like snakes;
A rustle of veins, tick of blood in the throat;
The lines of the face tangle and catch, and
A green leaf of language comes twisting out of her mouth.

The Liturgy

He has been invited to perform
The very ancient ceremony, the Farewell to Fire,
And with misgivings has agreed.

The day comes and doubt comes back.
He never thought his initiation
Would lead to this, he planned a quiet life
Studying the epigrams incised
On millennial plaques. And that
Is the reason he was asked to officiate;
The devotees in their casual search
Had spotted the sacred metal in his luggage.

He stands in the September afternoon glow, balancing
The copper shells and their ritual pouch in two hands,
Then clatters off down the stairs of the hostel.

They are waiting outside, the muffled band,
Their boat moored and loaded
With piled blankets, crocheted shawls,
Nets of mellowed fruit. Behind them,
The glitter of the estuary, the honeycomb
Of cliffs riddled with sunlight.

Meanwhile the house is empty
Except for the two women on the ground floor.
The latch of their room will never shut completely.
They hear the hinges of the big door closing,
They know the length of the ceremony, they know
They have just forty minutes.

History

Accept the gift
Ancestral flood
Parting the ground
Washing the living
Shearing the bank of ghosts —

These will not cauterise a wound.

The fire polluted you
With menstrual stain
Dirt from forges
Ashes fat and bones
From the invaders' feast.

The leaves of yellow metal
Were floated to us on the stream
Our grandmothers wrote in them
With reeds and vinegar —
That is a lost art

Our history is a mountain of salt
A leaking stain under the evening cliff
It will be gone in time
Grass will grow there —

Not in our time.

Observations from Galileo

1

If two such bodies are to touch each other
They will touch at one point only. This is plain
Though we do not know what they are, or if one
Looking like a dry fist of asphalt
Is in fact our tidal earth. Even so,
Over all her wild complexion there is only
One point where a man is proving, with basins of water
And sun reflected on a whitewashed wall,
As the servants draw long curtains back,
That such great bodies have their currents,
They feel corruption though they spell our time.

2

But who has not seen, in a city at night,
Returning home, how the moon jumps
From a gable to a high wall, keeps pace as you go,
Running along the rim of the wall like a cat?

Crossing

He thought his death near then, his life seemed
Like a drop within him, nearly at the dregs,
The stopper lost and the air sucking it dry.

I walked in the plantation with him and his grown children
To a graceful house burnt-out, Currah Chase,
Blunt on its eminence among the young spruce.

When we came to the neat locked gate
He climbed it without pausing, and we followed
His tracks to the ruin, its black windows lying

Open as the ornamental water below
To the *droit de seigneur* of the visiting swans —
The breeze rising, airing the cellars.

The Pig-boy

It was his bag of tricks she wanted, surely not him:
The pipkin that sat on the flame, its emissions
Transporting her so she skipped from kitchen to kitchen
Sampling licks of food; she knew who had bacon
And who had porridge and tea. And she needed
The swoop of light from his torch
That wavered as she walked,
Booted, through the evening fair,
Catching the green flash of sheeps' eyes,
The glow of false teeth in the skull:

Its grotto light stroked oxters of arches,
Bridges, lintels, probed cobbles of tunnels
Where the world shook itself inside out like a knitted sleeve:
Light on the frozen mesh, the fishbone curve, the threads
And weights.
                    And as day
Glittered on the skin, she stood
In the hood of a nostril and saw
The ocean gleam of his eye.

Permafrost Woman

Now, that face he coursed
Beyond all the lapping
Voices, through linear deserts

Unfolds among peaks
Of frozen sea, the wave
Coiling upward its wrinkled grace.

Dumb cliffs tell their story, split and reveal
Fathomed straits. The body opens its locks.

Spying the crowded
Ocean graveyard, wrecks shifting
A sea mile to the west as the blow falls,

The traveller feels
His hair bend at the fresh weight
Of snow, the wind is an intimate fist

Brushing back strands: he stares at the wide mouth, packed
With grinding ash: the landslide of his first dream.

Street

He fell in love with the butcher's daughter
When he saw her passing by in her white trousers
Dangling a knife on a ring at her belt.
He stared at the dark shining drops on the paving-stones.

One day he followed her
Down the slanting lane at the back of the shambles.
A door stood half-open
And the stairs were brushed and clean,
Her shoes paired on the bottom step,
Each tread marked with the red crescent
Her bare heels left, fading to faintest at the top.

The Hill-town

The bus floats away on the big road and leaves her
In sunlight, the only moving thing to be seen.

The girl at her kitchen-window in the ramparts
Can glimpse her through a steep rift between houses.
She turns to salt the boiling water
As her mother begins to climb, dark blue in the blue shade,
Past the shut doors and the open windows,
Their sounds of knife and glass.
She crosses into the sun before passing
The blank shutters of the glazier's house.

He is in there, has heard her step and
Paused, with the sharp tool in his hand.
He stands, his fingers pressed against the looking-glass
Like a man trying to hold up a falling building
That is not even a reflection now.

Their child knows where to glance, turning off the flame,
To spot her mother, a wrinkle in the light.
She remembers lying in the wide bed, three years old,
The sound of water and the gas going silent,
And the morning was in the white sieve of the curtain
Where a shadow moved, her mother's body, wet patches
Blotting the stretched cloth, shining like dawn.

Snow

'I thought of you then,' she says, 'flocking
On the edge of the same water —
The yearly walk by the banks — '
As she stood by the calm water
And the snow kept faltering past,
And past the window where a man's bare arm
Reached for clothes and for matches.

'I heard him calling,' she says; 'I stood there, planted,
Marking time.' She spotted, between the branches,
How the treecreeper survives by its own rites.
The beak tapped, the wedge of time sank.

She thought of them, crowding the cold shore
With pilgrimage, like migrant birds,
Their habitat a shrinking blot on the map,
The tidal ogham in their feathers
A message for the watcher, keeping score.

MacMoransbridge

Although the whole house creaks from their footsteps
The sisters, when he died,
Never hung up his dropped dressing-gown,
Took the ash from the grate, or opened his desk. His will,
Clearly marked, and left in the top drawer,
Is a litany of objects lost like itself.
The tarnished silver teapot, to be sold
And the money given to a niece for her music-lessons,
Is polished and used on Sundays. The rings and pendants
Devised by name to each dear sister are still
Tucked between silk scarves in his wardrobe, where he found
And hid them again, the day they buried his grandmother.
And his posthumous plan of slights and surprises
Has failed – though his bank account's frozen – to dam up time.

He had wanted it all to stop,
As he stopped moving between that room
With its diaries and letters posted abroad
And the cold office over the chemist's
Where he went to register deaths and births,

While the sisters went on as they do now, never
All resting at once – one of them would be
Boiling up mutton-shanks for broth, or washing out blankets,
Dipping her black clothes in boiled vitriol and oak-gall
(He used to see from his leafy window
Shoulders bobbing at the pump like pistons).
And still the youngest goes down at night to the stream,
Tending the salmon-nets at the weir,
And comes home to bed as the oldest of all
Can already be heard adding up small change with the servant.

Looking at the Fall

She stood again in the briar path,
Her child in her hand, and looked over
Where the water struck the rock, where
The divided leaf struck root, and saw
The shielded home of the spider surviving
Below the curve of the fall. She said,
What will it be when summer turns
The scapula to a dry bone?

Look, don't touch, she said to the reaching child.
Across her eye a shadow fell like a door closing upstream,
A lock slipping, a high stack of water
Loosed, spinning down, to slam them out of breath.

She looked again at the fall –
The rock half dry, the skein of water
Crooked and white – and saw
The ribs of a candle,
The flame blown adrift,
A draught from a warped door.

She looked at the rock and saw bone
And saw the bones piled in the mountainside
And the cross wind cutting at the roots,
Whistling in the dry bed of the stream.

Balloon

Let the child sleep now
The judge has finished, the papers are signed,
The cameras done flashing
On him as he held on tightly
To his lighter-than-air balloon.

Warm currents of his room
Shake the flagging lost balloon, revive
A floated search, coasting
From shelf, past open door, to rest
On a dance-floor, held and freed

By a loose jet of air.
Twisting the whiskered angles of toys,
Of musical instruments resting,
The silk lobe flutters not quite down to earth:
A big strange fish gleams, filling the child's bed.

London

At fifty, she misses the breast
That grew in her thirteenth year
And was removed last month. She misses
The small car she drove through the seaside town
And along cliffs for miles. In London
She will not take the tube, is afraid of taxis.

We choose a random bar. She sits by me,
Looking along the jacketed line of men's
Lunchtime backs, drinks her vermouth.
I see her eye slide to the left;
At the counter's end sits a high metal urn.

What are you staring at? That polished curve,
The glint wavering on steel, the features
Of our stranger neighbour distorted.
You can't see it from where you are.
When that streak of crooked light
Goes out, my life is over.

1981

River, with Boats

Of course she does not mind sleeping
On the deep fur of the bed
Beside the wide window
Where the birds hop,
Where the boats pass.

She can hear the hooters
Down there in a greeting;
She can see a flash of the river,
A glitter on the ceiling
When the wind blows
And the high branches of trees
On the other bank
Skip and bow in circles.

Only at the highest tide
The window is blocked
By the one framed eye
Of a tethered coaster
Swaying and tugging and flapping with the wind,
And the faces of the mariners
Crowd at the glass like fishes.

The Italian Kitchen

Time goes by the book laid open
On the long marble table: my work
In the kitchen your landlord painted yellow and white.
Beyond it the glass cupboard doors: behind them now
Ranged the green and yellow cups and plates
You bought in September and left behind, still in boxes.

One more of your suddenly furnished houses.
Eighteen years since we discovered, cash in hand,
Anonymous, the supermarket pleasures
Stacked and shinily wrapped, right
For this country, where all wipes clean,
Dries fast. Or California where you are now.

No sound from the man asleep upstairs.
At the hour's end I walk to the window
Looking over the slopes. Now the night mist
Rises off the vague plain, reaching
Our tall pine where cones cling like mussels:

Light still plays among the branches,
Touches the cold cheek of the window-pane.
I've bought blankets and firewood; we live here now.

Agello, March 1981

Recovery

A month since the hospital sleep
When I looked down on pain,
When dreams were riddled,
The pain could be a dream:
We sit so far away at a balcony table,
A succession of light dishes evolves
From salt to sweet, tasting of,
Trailing into the future, and we turn
To look down. The many-coloured women
Rinse and spread their light garments,
The river limps off between sandbanks
Yet turns a small millwheel.

A flight of steps shrugs down to the water-level,
Each one a pause, a window on the air,
The sun tangling cogs of light, the water
Angling at a small cloud
Never again to be so clearly seen.

Quarant' Ore

At the dark early hour
When the open door of the church
Is pumping out light,
The sacristan is at work unfolding
The stacked chairs, he carries them
Out of the porch, into the glow.
They spread wide like daisies,
They turn to the wide gold rose.
Follow it, ranked in rings.

And still it is not day
And the morning papers are lying
Dropped by gates in grey piles,
When the first pilgrims arrive,
Slipping into the dark shell of the porch,
To squat on the stone –
The practised knees doubled against the breastbone,
The elbows not interfering. They are packed
Lightly as drifted rubbish in corners.
They never obscure the blazing outline
Of the arch lying open for the real congregation
To roll up punctually in cars,
The knights with medals and white gloves.

A Voice

1

Having come this far, in response
To a woman's voice, a distant wailing,
Now he thinks he can distinguish words:
    You may come in –
    You are already in.

But the wall is thornbushes, crammed, barbed.
A human skeleton, warped in a dive, is clasped
In the grip of a flowery briar. His wincing flesh
Reproves him, turns and flows
Backwards like a tide.

2

Knowing it now for a trick of the light
He marches forward, takes account of
True stones and mortared walls,
Downfaces the shimmer
And shakes to hear the voice humming again:

In the bed of the stream
She lies in her bones –
Wide bearing hips and square
Elbows. Around them lodged,
Gravegoods of horsehair and an ebony peg.

'What sort of ornament is this?
What sort of mutilation? Where's
The muscle that called up the sound,
The tug of hair and the turned cheek?'
The sign persists, in the ridged fingerbone.

And he hears her voice, a wail of strings.

In Rome

The Pope's musketeers are breaking their fast
On the roof above my bed. Harsh burning of kebabs
Reeks down through the gap in the beams, and the retching
Of their caged doves. The captain lowered some charcoal
Last night; my poor girls are cooking eggs now
Behind the screen. Soon they must wrap
And veil up for the street, for the hours lounging
Nibbling bread in the Cardinal's front hall,
Twisting to keep their heels out of sight.

Then I have time to walk, alone on the carpet
On half the floor, where we eat and sleep together.
Not even the mice scramble on the clean boards.
We keep the bell-shrine there, and the gold chasubles
For the feast day. I must not go out.
But from the egg-shaped window
I can see the girls trailing back home, with a promise.

Indeed, only an hour after the markets close
The deaf runner from the palace climbs
With two silver pieces and odd coppers.
When we were at home it would have been three sheep –
Work for the troop, skinning, washing the guts,
Digging the pit for the fire. When the meat was eaten,
The wool to card and spin.
I am obliged to God for inventing the city,
To the Cardinal for the sound of money,
The clipped rounds, the battered profiles:
They circle my sleep like the faces of lost kin.

J'ai Mal à nos Dents

in memory of Anna Cullinane (Sister Mary Antony)

The Holy Father gave her leave
To return to her father's house
At seventy-eight years of age.

When young in the Franciscan house at Calais
She complained to the dentist, *I have a pain in our teeth*
– Her body dissolving out of her first mother,
Her five sisters aching at home.

Her brother listened to news
Five times in a morning on Radio Éireann
In Cork, as the Germans entered Calais.
Her name lay under the surface, he could not see her
Working all day with the sisters,
Stripping the hospital, loading the sick on lorries,
While Reverend Mother walked the wards and nourished them
With jugs of wine to hold their strength.
J'étais à moitié saoûle. It was done,
They lifted the old sisters on to the pig-cart
And the young walked out on the road to Desvres,
The wine still buzzing and the planes over their heads.

Je mangerai les pissenlits par les racines.
A year before she died she lost her French accent
Going home in her habit to care for her sister Nora
(Une malade à soigner une malade).
They handed her back her body,
Its voices and its death.

Consolation

His wife collects the rifled
Remains. The list accounted for,
His pockets emptied, their load (codes,
Lists, cards, his multiplied signature)
Locked up for her claiming,
It seems little was taken.
Between the pages of his passport
A copy of his deposition
Typed on the day of the incident, on a loud machine
By an irritated sergeant.

She asks the nun, 'But was that what killed him,
A blow on the head?' Alive,
Three days ago he asked the sergeant,
'What about the blow from behind?'
'No sir, the boy just landed from above you
    and snatched your wallet.'
'I felt it as a blow.'

He was still in the weavers' alley,
Turning to look past hanging cloth down an entry –
A burrow, green light at the end,
A sliver of an arch
Crossed by one trickling thread,
A segment of shoulder and arm –
And his shoulder felt the force, like a wall falling.

The hospital basement is vaulted and pillared:
A wide crypt, old and clean. The nun sits down
To rifle a desk for the right form of receipt.
'It was just as if he waited for the priest to come.'
'He was quite collected, he spoke sensibly.'

She hears the words, the repeated story:
There was no assassination, the fire in his brain
Came only from the red of the dyed cloth.
There was a pillared space when he was dying,
A voice and a response. It was not a hunt and a blow.

Fallen Tree in a Churchyard

in memoriam John Jordan

The tree falls, and
The daylight searches
Where once the roots
Discreetly moved one way
As a blind man's hand
Through a cat's coat.

The tangle, the drying clay
Coating the major passages
Never until now shaped
By flood or storm,
Becomes finally
Visible, halved
By the acute
Maker of threads, tier of knots,
Binder of air and earth:

We can see it now,
Forked and completed.

St Mary Magdalene Preaching at Marseilles

Now at the end of her life she is all hair –
A cataract flowing and freezing – and a voice
Breaking loose from the loose red hair,
The secret shroud of her skin:
A voice glittering in the wilderness.
She preaches in the city, she wanders
Late in the evening through shaded squares.

The hairs on the back of her wrists begin to lie down
And she breathes evenly, her elbows leaning
On a smooth wall. Down there in the piazza,
The boys are skimming on toy carts, warped
On their stomachs, like breathless fish.

She tucks her hair around her,
Looking beyond the game
To the suburban marshes.

Out there a shining traps the sun,
The waters are still clear,
Not a hook or a comma of ice
Holding them, the water-weeds
Lying collapsed like hair
At the turn of the tide;

They wait for the right time, then
Flip all together their thousands of sepia feet.

MUSE
INSPIRE

/

So She Looked, in that Company

Seeing her here
I know at once who she must be.
She does not move while
The pale figures out of the anthologies
In their coarse shirts are paraded
To tell their hesitant stories
Twisting the grammar of their exotic speech.

They line up as if
Back to the wall were the only possible stance.
Their throats are scarred and their voices
Birdlike.
               – Until the viewing is over,
The woman waits to be taken away,
Then they can be heard, heartily chatting
Among themselves, calling for big jugs of drink.

Chrissie

Escaped beyond hope, she climbs now
Back over the ribs of the wrecked ship,
Kneels on the crushed afterdeck, between gross
Maternal coils: the scaffolding
Surviving after pillage.
                    On the strand
The voices buzz and sink; heads can be seen
Ducking into hutches, bent over boiling pans.
The trees above the sand, like guests,
Range themselves, flounced, attentive.
Four notches down the sky, the sun gores the planks;
Light fills the growing cavity
That swells her, that ripens to her ending.

The tide returning shocks the keel;
The timbers gape again, meeting the salty breeze;
She lies where the wind rips at her left ear,
Her skirt flapping, the anchor-fluke
Biting her spine; she hears
The dull sounds from the island change
To a shrill evening cry. In her head she can see them
Pushing out boats, Mother Superior's shoulder to the stern
(Her tanned forehead more dreadful now
Than when helmeted and veiled)
                              And she goes on fingering
In the shallow split in the wood
The grandmother's charm, a stone once shaped like a walnut,
They had never found. Salt water soaked its force:
The beat of the oars cancelled its landward grace.

She clings, as once to the horned altar beside the well.

The Informant

Underneath the photograph
Of the old woman at her kitchen table
With a window beyond (fuchsias, a henhouse, the sea)
Are entered: her name and age, her late husband's
    occupation
(A gauger), her birthplace, not here
But in another parish, near the main road.
She is sitting with tea at her elbow
And her own fairy-cakes, baked that morning
For the young man who listens now to the tape
Of her voice changing, telling the story,
And hears himself asking,
Did you ever see it yourself?
                     Once, I saw it.

Can you describe it? But the sound
Takes off like a jet engine, the machine
Gone haywire, a tearing, an electric
Tempest. Then a stitch of silence.
Something has been lost, the voice resumes
Quietly now,
            'The locks
Forced upward, a shift of air
Pulled over the head. The face bent
And the eyes winced, like craning
To look in the core of a furnace.
The man unravelled
Back to a snag, a dark thread'.

Then what happens?
                    The person disappears.
For a time he stays close by and speaks
In a child's voice. He is not seen, and
You must leave food out for him, and be careful
Where you throw water after you wash your feet.

And then he is gone?
                    He's gone, after a while.

You find this more strange than the yearly miracle
Of the loaf turning into a child?
Well, that's natural, she says,
I often baked the bread for that myself.

A Whole Life

Down here it's sheltered, and the children play
Rolling down the grass bank
And always roll crooked; we look up;
The temple cranes out over the hill,
Seeming to fall as the wind flourishes, through
Arches opening on blanks, gallops up tumbles
Of crooked stairs, around pillars weathered,
Sucked by every breath that's blown here since the Fall.

Never equipped with a graveyard or a kitchen midden,
There's nothing to dig, the foundations
Are sand, the level flags are too smooth
To show a date; it faces every way.

– Along the skyline pass two black monks
Bearing a weighty book with an iron clasp.
They march between the arches and can still be seen.

Thus, after the lessons, the warnings
From the lady with the French pleat and the colonel's cap
– *Remember, you will have only one chance* –
The skills work to perfection, the parachute spreads,
The wind is a slide conveying the graceful soldier
To a landing on soft, crusted snow.

Those People

When the four women tramp in sight
Dragging their children round the corner,
All the dolls in the shop windows look askance.
The shopkeepers know these people,
They are not going to leave,
They will remain visible,
Still there at three in the afternoon
When the shops are closed and the bars
Shutter their darkness, they will be
Out on the cobbles, beside the abandoned
Slimy fountain, hardly moving at all
But showing no definite signs of sleep.
At night their campfire will glow
– They will be cooking that stew,
Lifting the lid to stir it, and
The smell will blow all over
As it reeks now from their skirts.

The man at the cash-register
Beside the looped bead curtain says
I think myself it's the goat's milk.

The Promise

In retrospect, it is all edge;
The rivers crossed were all one river, at the edge
Of a wide roughened patch, one like
The mark of a blow, a mark for life;
The road linked the twin towns, falling
In loops, like a shadow in water.

There, like a beckoning arm, a tree
Ventured a rounded branch between
Streetpacked façades; the air expanded,
Eyes shot wider, skin responded,
Fingers shuffled, hidden
Pianissimo, stroking the minted
Edge. So a grave-thief
Breathes deep and bristles, if
A bare coin gleams
Between pelvic rags, a profile
Warm from the pocket of Constantine.

In retrospect, it was all
A prelude to the embarkation.
I watch the bones, and they begin to shine,

Where, like a welded scar, we show
Where we have split and healed askew –

You rock inside your skin
Your bones rock in your flesh
The full bottles in the duty-free shop
Rattle like bells on the soft waves.

Nothing is going to happen until we land.